Misfits in the Front Row

Poems by

Sarah Worrel and James Benger

Spartan Press
Kansas City, Missouri
spartanpresskc.com

Copyright (c) Sarah Worrel, James Benger, 2021
First Edition 1 3 5 7 9 10 8 6 4 2
ISBN: 978-1-952411-55-7
LCCN: 2021932854

Cover image: Ruben Rodriguez
Title page image: Beniot Debaix
Author photos: Hannah Benger, Jeremey Worrel
All rights reserved. No part of this publication may be reproduced or transmitted in any form or by any means, electronic or mechanical, including photocopying, recording or by info retrieval system, without prior written permission from the author.

Sarah would like to thank James for being a stellar co-writer. She is grateful to Brian Daldorph, Linzi Garcia, Jason Baldinger, and Jeremy Gulley for providing helpful feedback. Sarah would also like to thank the family and friends who have put up with all this writing stuff for so long. Special thanks go to Kung Fu Treachery Press for giving this work a home.

James would like to thank Sarah for giving me the chance to write this book with her, and for Kung Fu Treachery Press for giving it a home, Jason Baldinger, Jeremy Gulley, Linzi Garcia, and Brian Daldorph for giving early versions of this book close readings and valuable feedback, all the people who show up in my poems here (many of the names have been changed), and as always, Dad, Hannah, Milo, and Felix.

Table of Contents

jccc, 2001 / 1

The KU Originals, 2011 / 3

tone / 4

Dude in math class / 5

write what they want you to know / 6

The kid in the back screwing with my studies / 7

angels and shotguns / 8

All the dead kids / 10

recess / 11

In grade school / 13

english class, 1997 / 14

English with Mr. T. / 16

invisible / 17

if only I could have been / 19

freshman bio / 20

Senior prank / 22

revolve / 23

lunchtime hurt / 25

greg / 26

In high school / 28

snowball / 30

had to pee / 32

critique / 33

hand-me-downs / 35

response / 36

lockers / 39

equal opportunity / 41

promised / 43

society / 44

excused / 46

assembly / 48

I had to learn lessons / 50

freedom / 53

so scared / 55

leak / 56

good intentions / 58

crack a window / 59

rumors / 60

overcast / 61

monotony / 63

near miss / 65

Jesus, God in heaven / 69

shop class / 70

first day / 72

For everyone who fell through the cracks, and for everyone who wanted to be left alone.

jccc, 2001
by James Benger

my eyes blur with last night's show;
the lasers were killer,
those naked acrobats from the rafters,
they had that shit locked down.

she's up at the board,
saying about group projects,
end-of-semester nonsense.

so here we is:
hungover,
wondering why we're doing this
half-assed higher education
that's destroying our savings,

wondering if that girl next to me
is actually into me,

wondering if i can get away
with inventing lab partners,
and research
and results,
'cause if i can lie,
i can have this done in ten minutes.

a couple buildings over,
there's coffee.

the library has jazz cds,
and back issues of rolling stone.

she's at the board saying:
p.h. balance.

the girl next to me,
she elbows my side,
says:
dude, why are you always so tired?

The KU Originals, 2011
by Sarah Worrel

started in a
writing class with
Brian Daldorph

when I asked James
if he was interested in
a writing group

because I was so
impressed with his
dedication to the craft
of writing

after reading some of
his work in one of
Daldorph's classes

been so long I
don't even remember if
it was poetry or fiction

I didn't know anything else about
him
what kind of student he was or
wasn't but I knew that he
made the time to
write in a way I never had

tone
by James Benger

working a split at the gas station
so i can hit up a mid-morning class
in between.

my torn jeans smell like
burned coffee and spilled gas,
and my eyes are still blurry
from the night before.

other professor's holding class over;
test or something,
so i congregate with my classmates
in the hallway.

stoner dude with the dirty hair
and the zeppelin t-shirt sidles up,
asks if i know how to get that
mid-seventies brad whitford tone.

thinking about the rest of the
workday ahead of me,
thinking daggers at last night's rum,
in no mood for conversation,
i say:
with your fingers, man,
the tone's in your fingers.

Dude in math class
by Sarah Worrel

always wore his
Zoso
shirt—
at least weekly

and I never knew
what it meant until
I looked it up
just now—
over two decades
later—and it
doesn't mean anything
to anyone
except Jimmy Page
and other
Zepheads

write what they want you to know
by James Benger

college freshman composition class,
i turn in my paper
in which i quote
a john lennon biography,
and the liner notes
to *incesticide*.

as asked, i provide
photocopies of my sources,
photocopies which cost me
my last handful of dimes
at the library xerox.

professor gives my theme
a cursory glance,
no doubt, he's already
seen too many.
then he hands it back
with red ink that says:

c-

…try harder.

The kid in the back screwing with my studies
by Sarah Worrel

knows he can't
shut up

he told
the professor so

gave her
permission
to cut off
his words

but she's
too
polite

I'm paying for
professors

not that
kid in the back who
can't keep
his mouth shut

angels and shotguns
by James Benger

old jacobson, with his thick,
vaguely eastern european accent
got on the intercom
before the usual leading
of the pledge of allegiance.
he hitchingly read some poem
about angels and better places.

old widow hara was up by the board--
by the flag--ready for what was next,
but she had a tear in her eye,
barely concealed sniffles.

turns out that boy one grade up--
the kid i sometimes raced at recess,
batted kickballs around--
he had an older brother
who had a birthday.
birthday boy's grandpappy
got him his own shotgun.

now that boy a grade up from me,
he wouldn't be going to school
or anywhere else.

the lunchroom served
room temperature pizza that day,
and i couldn't understand
why we were bothering with any of it.

All the dead kids
by Sarah Worrel

I ever knew
were eclipsed

by the pain I
saw
working at Olathe Northwest

when two girls
in one week

killed
themselves

recess
by James Benger

we would find spent cigarette butts
left by the older kids,
and maybe some teachers too.
someone always had a lighter,
when no one was looking,
we'd light the butts up;
they were usually
good for a hit or two.
it made us feel
grownup, cool, real,
more than just dumb kids.

once we found a discarded
fast food batman toy,
and chucked it into the
wastewater pit.
watching it sink,
we pretended it was
jack nicholson.

those were the hot days
when sweat would
mingle with blood
in the dusty gravel
of the dugout,

but we never
thought much of it,
because the sun always screamed
the scorching promise
of tomorrow.

In grade school
by Sarah Worrel

there was a cement
storm drain with
manhole cover

that was an excellent spot
to play pretend

howl like wolves
be alien princesses

and not get made fun of
by the popular kids

english class, 1997
by James Benger

josh's parents got him a cellular phone,
but much like baseball caps,
and earrings on boys,
it wasn't allowed in class.

i was pretty sure sam dug me,
and she was cute,
in a hairspray queen sort of way,
but she was regularly dickish
to joey, who was slow
and socially awkward,
but was a nice enough guy.

jared swore his sideburns were
cooler than elvis,
and certainly cooler than me.

mr. w. sat in front of the class
and hit on all the girls in the front row
who filled out their sweaters to his liking.

weird larry pointed at me,
said that long hair was a sin.

jared asked:
what about jesus?

larry said:
not my jesus.

josh's cell rang,
mr. w. gave me a c
for my report on a book
i didn't read,
and i never found out
what sam looked like naked.

English with Mr. T.
by Sarah Worrel

he was phoning it in
waiting for retirement
and everyone
knew it

we worked on a poem by
Dickinson and everybody looked
to me
for the answers

but when we finished
I could hear them talking about
me

about the slumber party where I
asked a stupid hypothetical question
because I felt safe

nobody in the classroom had been
there
so the rumors spread fast

and Mr. T. either
didn't hear
or didn't care
about how shitty the other
kids
were being

invisible
by James Benger

old widow hara
brought supplies in
an old osco drug plastic sack.
picking my pipecleaners
and colors of construction paper,
and whatnot,
i wondered if nancy reagan
was all just say no,
and she was in bed with the president,
why would a company
put 'drug' right on the bag?
and how does an old, doddering teacher
get away with bringing said bag
to a room full of kids?

i was thinking these things
back at my desk, rounded scissors,
and weirdly disconcerting paste pot;
what with a cow on the label,
cartoon representation of
what the paste used to be,
i was thinking these things as
hara said stuff about
never go anywhere
without a grownup,
and i absentmindedly
punched a staple right into my thumb.

the pain was immediate, hot,
but what was more was the fear,
wondering how much trouble
i would get into for being so careless.

as she was up there,
her speech going on and on and on,
scissors scritching the paper,
i snuck to the bathroom.

there in the silence down the hall,
i stuck the little bit of staple that was
outside the skin between my teeth,
and pulled.

spitting the bloody thing in the sink,
wrapping my thumb in a
scratchy paper towel,
i wondered what kind of
hell i'd be in,
leaving the room
without a grownup,
or even permission.

i got back,
snuck to my seat.

no one noticed.

and that was the first time
i was glad i was invisible.

if only I could have been
by Sarah Worrel

invisible
when I would overhear
other students talking about
my fashion choices

and how I *gasp*
wore biker shorts with
t-shirts that didn't cover my
butt

or that one flowery shirt
that admittedly looked like
a Mom shirt

or how foot traffic would get
backed up in the hallways and I'd
be too close and going too fast to just
stop
so I'd tiptoe to keep from running into
another person—
which would be rude

instead of being invisible I
probably had
tomato red
cheeks

freshman bio
by James Benger

we had this bio teacher,
was retiring mid-year,
so he really didn't
give much of a shit.
he taught us okay,
was certainly compassionate,
but i can't say i
learned a whole lot about biology.

we were given frogs to
dissect, pin, and label.
i still got a b after
turning my amphibian
into a puppet,
and making him do that dance
the frog in the old warner brothers cartoons did,
which made my lab partner, cody
shoot fruitopia out of his nose.

the whole room smelled like
formaldehyde and mediocrity.
the stench would get in your nose
and not leave for hours.

i had lunch after bio.
no matter how you doctored it,

that bland, soggy rectangle pizza
always smelled like how one would imagine
preserved pig fetuses tasted.

freshman bio caused me to
skip eating a lot of lunches,
but cody and i,
we knew the words
and most of the chords
to nearly every nirvana song,
and we really didn't care,
and our teacher was pretty lax,
so maybe it wasn't that bad.

Senior prank
by Sarah Worrel

during lunch
someone set off smoke
bombs

kids with asthma
couldn't breathe

and all I could think about
was being
hungry

cause I was 15
and an asshole

so my girlfriend and
I got a hold of my mom
to bring us pizza

and one of the teachers
was so pissed that
we didn't think of anyone else
but ourselves
she reamed me out

but I got to eat my
fucking
pizza

revolve
by James Benger

junior lit, all salinger and shakespeare,
out in that trailer
gloriously dubbed 'the mobile,'
heater never quite worked,
so gloves and hats
were the usual,
someone called in a bomb threat.

it was spring, though,
so no cold weather gear,
but it was also
a week after columbine.

everyone blamed/lauded
the goth kid who
always wore a trenchcoat.
he got brought in for questioning
after the fact.
spoiler: it wasn't him.

what i remember most
was the whole school
walking single-file
down the farm road
to the elementary school,
where we holed up in the
auditorium for hours
until the all-clear.

none of us had cell phones,
and few of us had quarters,
so not a lot of calls went
to parents that day.

my future roommate and i,
we snuck to the music room,
jammed some doom metal
on elementary instruments,
but all i could think about was
the portable cd player
in my backpack,
back in the mobile,
that may or may not have
exploded.

lunchtime hurt
by Sarah Worrel

it was the week of the dance—
which one doesn't matter—
and I borrowed one of
Mom's dresses that
made my tits look
amazing

one of my friends asked
if I was trying to
get a date for the dance
so apparently my efforts were
over-the-top obvious
cause it was one
of my guy friends

I should have asked Mom for
permission to wear the dress
if she's said no
she might have
saved
me from crying in the
bathroom at lunchtime

greg
by James Benger

greg never talked much,
had glasses so thick,
you couldn't ever be sure
which way he was looking.
we never knew much
about greg's home life,
but we all wondered,
and speculated.

freshman algebra,
he sat silent in class
while i tried to
make the moves on
the girl with the
ironic t-shirt,
which as it turned out,
wasn't all that ironic;
she really was that into
jesus and punishing the unbelievers.

sometime during that semester,
the cops came,
hauled greg out of the room.
seems greg had
quite the stash in his locker,
complete with one of the most
massive bongs anyone had ever seen.

the next day when i found out,
i mused on how
greg really was a
guy i should've known.

In high school
by Sarah Worrel

there was this
guy
who sold drugs
they said

but I never knew
one way or the other

somehow years later I
ended up at his place with
his girlfriend or wife—I
can't remember which—
she didn't like the way I
was sitting with my
ex-boyfriend

his arm
wrapped around me
when he already had
a girlfriend who wasn't me

and later he found out
who I gave my
virginity to and he
was so stinking jealous that he
wasn't the first one to get
in my pants

but when we'd make out in his
bedroom in the basement
he'd let his younger siblings
watch

I found out later
and I was so glad I
never let it get anywhere
close to that far

snowball
by James Benger

call me innocent,
or just plain naïve,
but until that evening,
i didn't know what it meant.

at the tail end of high school
we were all slackers,
just enough to get by,
always thinking of
the next release.

the senior wing was
for little more than slacking;
was practically an
airport lounge.

we sat on the floor
by our lockers,
talking shit,
trading tapes.

that rocker chick,
the one i was
forever friend-zoned with,
she flashes our band's cassette,
says:

"dude, you guys are
gonna be fuckin famous!"

that night we're in the basement,
we jam for a while,
but it turns to
eating pizza,
drinking beer,
watching a bootleg concert
on vhs on the twelve-inch.

while no one's looking,
someone changes the tape
for porn,
and then i know.

had to pee
by Sarah Worrel

and the smoker's bathroom was
closest
I should have known
the assistant principal was
doing random checks
but nobody told me

so Ms. P. tried to bust
me for smoking—
but she didn't understand
the culture
the rules

smokers used the
stalls at the far end
legit users went
in stalls near the door

one of the smokers actually
stood up for me
said I wasn't doing
anything

critique
by James Benger

first grade, sitting on the can,
red and white mickey mouse
underwear that was probably
first worn sometime
in the late seventies.

there was this bigger kid,
a fifth-grader, i think,
had seen him trolling
the trailer park on the
north end of town,
looking for stray cats to torture.

he comes in to bleed the dragon
against the wall-length urinal.
after, i hear the snick of a lighter,
then a pause.
big kid gets on all fours,
patrolling under stall doors,
making sure there are no witnesses.

of course i don't know enough
to lift my legs.

big kid, he hops up,
hangs from the top of the stall,
peers down, sees my underwear,
snickers and says:

fool's wearing mickey mouse!
fuckin fag!

then he drops down,
leaves me alone in the bathroom
to contemplate that word,
which though i didn't know the meaning,
i was pretty sure it wasn't a compliment.

hand-me-downs
by Sarah Worrel

we practiced sustainability before
it was even part of the conversation

I wore the clothes the daughter of the bus driver had
worn

one sweater in particular I
adored
black with diamonds in rainbow
shades
or maybe neon. I
don't remember, but it
was bold
and beautiful

and not cool

response
by James Benger

we had these shitty half-sized lockers
which were handed down from
some high school that went bust
in the sixties,
built-in locks. in orientation
it was boasted that we wouldn't
have to visit the hardware store
on our own dime.

despite these cries of
economical convenience,
my locker was constantly
giving me hell.

dr. r., the dean, was known
for patrolling the halls
during passing periods,
busting anyone for anything.
she especially had it out
for the guys.
most kids referred to dr. r.
as dr. d.; the d standing for a
derogatory name based on
her short hair, broad shoulders,
and deep voice.
the boys tended to be more vocal

with their calling her this,
which might explain her predilection
for popping any guy for anything.

one shitty day,
i'm fighting my locker,
it won't open,
it won't open,
it won't fucking open.
i kick it
hard.
hard enough to put a dent
in the purple aluminum door.
i reach back to deliver
one hell of a right.
my arm fully extended behind me,
dr. r. grabs my wrist.

towering over me, she booms
in her graveyard voice:

what the hell do you think you're doing?

i don't reply, somewhere between
rage and shock.

still holding my wrist,
practically twisting it behind my back,
she continues:

it doesn't respond to being hit.

how would you like it
if i hauled off and hit you?
would you respond?

i gave her an answer then:

you're fuckin a i'd respond to being hit.

dr. r. gets this shocked look on her face,
lets go of my arm,
and walks away,
quickly heading toward her office
down the hall.

massaging my recently overtaxed shoulder,
i kick my locker again.

it opens.

lockers
by Sarah Worrel

were a torment
because you only had
six minutes for
passing period
and if you happened to be
constipated
there was no
fucking
way you'd be to class
on time

and once I even missed
the bus along with
Donald
I think
but it's been so long
that I'm not sure if he would
even remember now

so they sent us a short bus

and I quit putting books in
my locker
and started carrying a tote on
one shoulder
and developed back problems

because of how torqued my
neck was from carrying all those
books that way

because Mz. F. wasn't going to
excuse me for being constipated
like how do you even ask for
permission to go? Why should
you?

and now I'm more tightly
strung than ever and
more likely to have
the runs than anything else
because IBS

and my mom keeps suggesting
I take an over-the-counter med
to stop it
but it seems like it either runs
or I'm stopped up
and there is no winning this

equal opportunity
by James Benger

in an effort at fairness,
they'd cram the boys into
the home ec classes
with the girls.

the rooms were never made
to hold that many children,
but we sweaty adolescent males
didn't much mind
being pressed up to
and forced into lab situations with
girls who would otherwise
never give us the time of day.

no one cared about that class;
it was like shop
only it felt significantly more pointless.

vanessa laughed when i managed to burn
our group's english muffin pizzas
to something blacker than
the charcoal in art class.
the elderly teacher with braces
shook her head,
told me to clean up.

lacy thought it was hilarious
that i couldn't thread a sewing machine
to save my life.
many times i came close
to giving myself stitches.
i still have no idea
what the hell a bobbin is.

when i presented my final project:
a sweatshirt, which despite her best efforts,
mom couldn't make serviceable,
the teacher gave me a c-,
but the class gave me
a laughing approval.

corrie said:
 "you'd be cute,
if your hair wasn't so long."

promised
by Sarah Worrel

they told us we could be
anything

president
CEO

the glass ceiling was
shattering

they told us we could have
everything

the job
kids

they never told us we needed
to make choices

a successful Mom might not be
a successful business woman and
vice versa

we were spoon-fed lies and that was
decades ago

there are still glass ceilings
there are still choices

society
by James Benger

somewhere between the
health class video
where that one girl
vomited at the sight
of afterbirth,

and that long, long speech
from the vice principal
about the evils of drugs,
which he shot at us
with his two-packs-a-day breath,
and all those empties
rolling around the bed of his truck,

somewhere between those,
they had someone
claiming to be a financial expert
(i'm not convinced she wasn't
a rookie bank teller)
come in and talk on
the importance of
balancing one's checkbook daily,
and making sure to
get a credit card
as soon as was legal,
only to build credit, of course.

it was an endless lecture
on financial responsibility,
which if she was to believed,
was key to being a
functioning part of society.

squirming in my thin wooden desk,
i reflected on my parents' house,
built in the 1930s,
not originally equipped with
a bathroom or electricity,
that little green box,
the bank note balance,
i would surely inherit.
thinking on that,
i found society lacking;

falling off the grid
never sounded more appealing,
and i often fantasized about
a life out in the woods,
just me and nature.

seemed to me,
all society ever gave anyone
was a two-pack-a-day habit,
a truck bed full of empties,
and some bloody jelly on the floor.

excused
by Sarah Worrel

if possible, from any
and all school assemblies
because I don't do sports
I'm not friends with the jocks

so assemblies were always
an exercise in boredom
celebrating athletes and
their wins at the big game

watching the cheerleaders,
color guard, and
band
all celebrate and
make much of sport
when we were an
academic institution—
I thought—
so when do we celebrate those
oh, just once at graduation
okay

I got stuck at a surprise
assembly once
couldn't get excused by
my mom fast enough

it was about STDs and showed
pictures of diseased organs
that I can't make sense of
even decades later
because at the time I had no idea
what healthy male organs even looked like

and my friend S. tried to keep me
from looking when all I wanted
was to figure out what was the frank
which were the beans and what
was wrong with the whole picture

pretty sure that was the only
assembly I wasn't bored at

totally uncomfortable the entire time

assembly
by James Benger

any excuse to not be
in class,
not caring,
always edging on
nodding off.

so it was alright,
in then lamest definition
of alright.

most times
we were supposed to sit
in assigned spots,
but i usually snuck off
to find ricky.

ricky rode the short bus,
spent all day locked away
in the l.d. room,
what a lot of the kids called
"a hard r."
he could barely speak,
it was hard to pick out
his words at first,
but over time you could read him
without speech,
and that was something greater.

he was always sitting there
on those blonde bleachers,
smiling away at the spectacle.
the pep band would kick in,
and while the gym would
inevitably, perfunctorily
clap on the downbeat,
ricky had the funkiest sense of rhythm;
would find the coolest,
most intricate polyrhythms.

i'd study his hands,
his feet,
doing my feeble best to learn
in a way that never
caught me in any class.

that senior, will, was in
the pep band,
and normally a horn dude,
every once in a while
they'd let him plug in his bass.
one time he busted out
that chili peppers song, warped,
to a standing ovation.

ricky found all the funk in that.

while maybe not the
best part of school,
it wasn't half bad
if you didn't really care.

I had to learn lessons
by Sarah Worrel

in not caring so much
like the time I
hadn't finished my homework and
asked Donald to see his and
check my answers
but really to copy them

and Mrs. M. freaked
because Donald was going
into the Air Force and
this could get him kicked out
before he'd even started if
he knew what I was doing
but he didn't

and my slacker friend
told me it was better to just take
the F
obviously
over all
the trouble I'd just caused

and then there was the time I
was so eager to see the rest of the movie that
I rented it and watched it at home
and skipped the next day of class

because I'd already seen it
and I guess Mrs. M. thought she
was going to fucking bust me for
not doing shit
cause she assigned an essay

that I heard about the day after the
period I skipped

and I wished I'd been there to
start thinking about how to write the
essay
cause she assigned it the day I
skipped

and she hated that I
always had an excuse note for
assemblies
because these kids were my friends
she said
I should be supporting them
and all I can think to myself
is which fucking kids is she talking about
my five friends in band
because none of my other friends were joiners
either

and weren't jocks
weren't cheerleaders
maybe one or two was in color guard the

entirety of high school
and yeah
I was on the swim team
but nobody gave a shit about swim team
except the people on swim team

and when it came time for NHS applications
I went straight to Mrs. M.
because I knew she'd deny my
application
along with Mr. M. — no relation—
because they were the two teachers I'd
impressed least in my entire high school
career
and I didn't want to do all that volunteering shit
because I was too busy smoking at
Hardee's all those periods I skipped
and hanging out with my cool
older friends
who in retrospect were
not so cool
being drug dealers
and all

freedom
by James Benger

for some strange reason,
every once in a while
they'd treat us with respect,
like we were adults,
like we were people,
and not the cows in the chute
that we so obviously were.

lunch hour was for leeway;
the kids who stayed
could go out to the courtyard,
that grandiosely named
few square yards of green
surrounded by brick,
cracked birdbath in the middle,
so they could smoke
and look some approximation of cool.

the rest of us,
they'd let us go
as far as across the streets,
either of them.

so we had a choice between
a mom and pop pizza place,
which meant you had to

walk across a busy road,
cars for hours, and whatever the speed limit,
no one cared, especially not us
when we finally got cars,

or a tiny gas station,
where we only had to
cross a cracked lane,
and they had beer and
didn't card.

we came back
bad breath and buzzed
almost every day.

dad worked in the factory
across the wire fence
from our school.

one day one of his coworkers
got busted for meth,
and there was talk of
not letting students
leave campus at lunch anymore.

but we moved at the
end of the semester,
so i don't know how that turned out.

so scared
by Sarah Worrel

of cars at
the busy four-way intersection of
Blackbob & 143rd St. long before
it had streetlights

I'd walk up Blackbob nearly to the cemetery some days
just so I
could account for two lanes of
traffic and not asshole drivers coming
from all four directions

back when Blackbob didn't even
have sidewalks there and Mrs. C. fought
for me
for us
to get free bus
because I was such an anxious
freak

leak
by James Benger

beater down again,
i was in the back of the bus,
listening to it all,
and not wanting any of it.

there was a weird,
pervasive smell
in the air that morning.

dick, old wwii vet
drove the bus,
insisted we blast
hi-99, the c&w station
every morning.

as we crawled into the
potholed lot of
north high school,
dj came on,
said another nerve gas leak
at the supposedly decommissioned
munitions plant
just outside of town,
said it was probably nothing
to get your shorts in a twist about,
but maybe stay inside today.

we walked into school,
a little dazed, a little scared,
but not much more.

took a week to
get the smell out of our noses.

good intentions
by Sarah Worrel

sat in the back of
the bus for the first
time in grade school

not knowing it was the
bully's seat and he
wasn't pleased, saying so
with much cursing

being a prudish Christian
I told him that he
shouldn't talk like that

and found myself
abandoning all those
good intentions just
a few years later

crack a window

by James Benger

we would roll
with the windows open
so we could
yell at the cows in the fields
between home and school.
and so some could smoke.

josh got kicked out of
fifth grade for smoking crack
on the morning bus ride.

when grandma asked
why he hadn't
been round much lately,
first i told her
he got kicked out for drugs.

grandma gave a
knowing smile.
then i told her the
whole deal.

her eyes got wide,
then she muttered:
jesus, whatever happened
to smoking pot?
you kids are taking it too far
these days.

rumors
by Sarah Worrel

flew fast about
the girl who puked or
passed out in class
(I can't remember which anymore,
but it doesn't much matter)

she'd had vodka in
her water bottle

I thought I hated
school
but she had to drink herself
senseless to get through the day

overcast
by James Benger

there were the bland days,
the monotonous nothing days,
the ones where everything repeated,
and nothing made sense,
and nothing ever seemed to matter.
the world,
everything.
everyone seemed so hopeless.

after the bus dropped me off
in the middle of the complex,
i'd try to hide in my room
in that little third floor apartment
on state line,
headphones on,
listening to my metallica,
or nirvana,
or beatles tapes.

but even that wouldn't do it;
wouldn't shake the
pointlessness,
wouldn't shake the fact that
people kept telling me
it was the best years of my life,
couldn't rinse that
from my ripped-out jeans.

there was a drainage pipe
at the edge of the complex,
if you followed it enough,
you'd end in a pretty good
stretch of woods.

mom at work,
dad sleeping off the night shift,
how'd that education work out for them?
brother and sister were
fine with cartoons on vhs,
they'd soon know what i was learning,
i'd raid the kitchen,
take a couple few beers,
or maybe some brandy,
follow that pipe to the
mosquito woods.

as the sun went red,
and i walked back,
nothing seemed less hopeless,
pointless, grey,
but at that moment,
it seemed tolerable,
and i thought:

maybe this is what adulthood is;
tolerating the grey
until the black finally comes.

monotony
by Sarah Worrel

of the grape pb&j sandwiches on
wheat bread any time I didn't want
the school lunch

and now I have to have crunchy sunbutter
and raspberry or strawberry jelly or anything besides
grape

no more gluten
no more peanut butter
sunbutter is okay
but bread without gluten doesn't
seem like bread at all

and the one time Dad made lunch
because Mom was birthing little
sister
or something
I don't remember
he put country crock shedd's spread on
my pb&j, later said something about nuns doing
it to keep kids from choking

I still don't know what nuns he was talking about
they weren't Catholic nor did he go to Catholic school
I wonder if he'd tell me

or if it'd be like asking about Korea and serving
overseas and how he won't talk about it
but I know at one point that he wanted to
die and if he hadn't had Mom & I back home
he would have probably eaten his gun

near miss
by James Benger

we had clubs,
we called them gangs
out on the playground.
whatever the flavor of the week was,
that was what we were.

we were a bit violent,
always fighting,
fighting
with the rival gangs.
the rivalries were
almost always mismatched.

gearing up for the new
michael keaton movie,
tv had been showing the
old adam west show on
infinite repeat.
we were the batman gang.
we took turns,
but most days,
i was batman.

one winter day on the playground,
we picked a fight
with the carebear gang.

i know...
this ended with me and steph
(the girl my younger brother dug)
wrestling in the sand pit.
no one drew blood,
and in fact we were laughing
(the fights were always
kinda jokes to the ones
doing the fighting),
but somehow we managed to
rip the hoods off
each other's coats.

recess monitor jerked us both up
by our scruffs,
one in each fist, she tells us:

you in some shit now!

steph and i, we stood outside
old man jacobson's office,
waiting to be sentenced.

steph grabs my hand, says:

my mom can't know,
i just can't take another beating.

i told her:

don't worry, i'll get us out of this,

hoping i sounded more confident
than i felt.

terry, the blond upperclassman
who lived in the trailer
down the road from our place,
he walked out of the office
with a shit-eating grin,
but he was rubbing his blue jeaned ass.

jacobson shouts through the open door:

get in here you two!

we go in,
i close the door behind us.
the paddle on the wall
is still swinging from its nail.

the principal stares at us, says:

well, why are you here?

steph and i,
we hold up our coats in concert.

he puts his head in his hands, says:

jesus.
i don't have the energy for this.
recess is almost over,
just go to class.

steph and i knew
we'd dodged a bullet,
and should be skipping,
but we walked in silence
to the other side of the school
holding hands.

her fingers were trembling.

Jesus, God in heaven
by Sarah Worrel

not sure how old I was
probably elementary school and
my dad busted my ass with a fucking
paint stir

you know those plastic whippy tools with holes in them—
but if I was really unlucky, on a bad
day
dad'd bust my ass with his fucking leather belt

shop class
by James Benger

first day of shop class,
teacher looms behind his desk,
tells us all:

i work out every day,
so don't fuck with me.
and i shower twice a day,
so don't you ever
say i stink!
and if you see me in
the boy's locker room,
you better show
some goddamned respect.

we had hardly sat down,
opened our notebooks,
mechanical pencils
not even at the ready.

we'd had fantasies of
insanely intricate
things of wood,
kept dreaming of
magnificent blueprints.

teacher dug at the
crotch of his jeans
with a pencil and said:

if you shits behave,
i'll show you how to make
a camera out of a
coffee can.

first day
by Sarah Worrel

of the semester at KU that
I'm on the right meds for the first
time and the whole world feels
like exciting possibility

fluffy clouds
unicorns
rainbows
and hope

Sarah Worrel's poems have appeared at *150kansaspoems, The Daily Drunk, Winedrunk Sidewalk: Shipwrecked in Trumpland,* and in *365 Days: A Poetry Anthology vol. 1 & vol. 2* with more in *vol. 3*. Her short stories are in *Coal City Review* and *James Gunn's Ad Astra*. She wades through JCCC bureaucracy in the Writing Center and in Fashion Design classes far too often for her liking.

James Benger is the author of two fiction e-books, and three chapbooks, two full-lengths, and coauthor of three other split books of poetry. He is on the Board of Directors for The Writers Place and the Riverfront Readings Committee, and is the founder of the 365 Poems In 365 Days online workshop, and is Editor in chief of the subsequent anthology series. He lives in Kansas City with his wife and children.